25 Plus Proven Ways To Make More Money In Your Home Watch Business

(While making your clients fiercely loyal!)

Mark Mehling

"The Home Watch Guy"

AUTHOR INSIGHT
SCAN WITH SMARTPHONE
or GO TO http://bit.ly/1c1ecod

The 39PageGuide *series is your shortcut to expert information. You could spend hours searching the web and still not find the information you have here in a simple, easy to read, short summary.*

Each book provides a solid foundation that saves you a ton of time and fruitless hunting. The books are at least 39 pages, some as many as 80 pages.

Keep in mind our goal:

- *Easy to read, less than 2 hours for the average reader*
- *At least 36 pages of information*
- *Quick to understand, distilled to be readable and informative immediately*
- *Written by an expert for those with little or no knowledge.*
- *More than an overview but less than a compendium*
- *An offer for more information from the author (optional)*

If you want to get to the meat of a topic quickly, 39pageguidebooks *make that happen.*

If you like fat filled, long explanations, 'technical jargon', and lots of space used up by 'pretty' pictures, at 3 times the price, these books are NOT for you.

Legal Stuff

Are you a lawyer? I am not either. Nor am I an accountant or tax expert. So nothing you read here should be construed or interpreted as legal, accounting, or tax advice. By purchasing and reading this book, you acknowledge that I am not responsible for your actions taken based on what you read here. Yes, you are accountable. If there is any doubt about anything in this book, consult an appropriately trained professional to ensure you are not doing anything illegal.

How to use this book

This book is divided into three sections:

1. Additional **SERVICES** you can offer
2. Other **PRODUCTS** you can offer
3. **COMBINATIONS** and Long Term Moneymakers

You can pick and choose, implement one or all.

I do recommend reading all of the ideas at least once.

NOTES:

TABLE OF CONTENTS

OTHER BOOKS AND RESOURCES FROM THE AUTHOR:

- *Leaving Your Home-ALONE* - A step-by-step guide to leaving your property empty for months at a time.
- *17 Days to Your Own Profitable Home Watch Business* - A guide to establishing your own business in less than 3 weeks

Both available on Amazon.com

LOOK FOR THESE ADDITIONAL RESOURCES SOON:

BOOKS:

- *Blow Away the Competition in Your Home Watch Business*

CDs/DVDs:

- DVD101: HomeWatchValet's Award Winning Marketing
-

- DVD102: Every Checklist/Form for Any Home Watch Situation
-

  DVD103: Every Tool I Use - and Why

Order form at the end of the book.

If you would like notice of future books and CDs, send an email to the author at Mark@TakeControlMarketing.com.

Your email will only be used to notify you when new products are available and will not be used or sold for any other purpose.

INTRODUCTION

Owning your own home watch business can be a profitable and fun way to supplement your income and has the potential to be a full time career move. But many home watch business owners forget that there are only 3 ways to increase your income in this, or any business:

1. Get more customers
2. Get existing customers to buy more
3. Get existing customers to buy more frequently.

Most home watch businesses focus only on the first point- getting more customers. This guide is about the second and third points- getting your existing customers to buy more, and more often. Your customer list is a rich source of possible sales above and beyond the minimum service.

Your clients want to use you to solve their problems. They already know you, trust you (hopefully) and hate the risk of trying out someone else and then getting hosed.

How do I know? I am the founder of Home Watch Valet, one of the oldest established home watch services. Also known as "TheHomeWatchGuy," I wrote the book for snowbirds titled, *Leaving Your Home-ALONE,* (available on Amazon.com and an excellent resource for anyone considering the business). My staff and I pioneered some of the early ideas of how to offer this service.

I have made all the mistakes. Hit the home runs, and occasionally struck out. Now I am sharing what I have learned with you. There are several books, currently in print or soon to be released, that are part of this series.

My most recent book, *17 Days to Your Own Profitable Home Watch Business,* is already doing well. So this book is aimed at those who have started a business but have not seen the profits they anticipated. This book will show you how to leverage the position you already hold, your clients' confidence, trust, and property access, to bring in more profits.

This short book is about ways to increase your profits considering:

- *You already have the customer (no additional marketing costs there)*
- *You are already going out to the house (no additional driving expense)*

- *You are already doing the billing (no additional effort there)*

This book is not long, but has many ideas that can make your business grow more profitably even with the number of clients you already have. There are additional resources available in the back for those who really want to make this a lasting, and serious, business.

This guide is written for the serious business owner. These are proven tactics that will make more profit. But they will take an effort to implement.

NOTES:

AUTHOR INSIGHT
SCAN WITH SMARTPHONE

or GO TO http://bit.ly/1a184GV

SECTION 1: ADDITIONAL SERVICES

The reason snowbirds have hired you to manage their property is simple and basic—they don't want the hassle of coming home to surprises and messes. You can leverage those feelings into profit in many other areas by offering services that make coming home a happier experience!

PRESSURE WASHING

If you live in the south, you already know how black driveways and houses get from mold. Houses up north get dirty from the blowing snow, rain and filth.

There is a reason pressure washers (machines as well as services) are so easily available. Everyone needs the cleaning they can give—at least once and sometimes twice a year.

NOTE: This is one of the tasks you may choose to do yourself. Here's a simple killer marketing idea if you choose to do it yourself: Use a 'sandwich board' large sign when you work that says "Ask me for a quote!" in large letters. I guarantee cars will stop! Have your business cards ready!

Twice a year, I send a note out in my newsletter, as well as in the mail, asking my clients to contact me if they need pressure-washing services. Once I have everyone's needs, I contact three providers and ask them to quote prices for every house, knowing they will get all or none.

Most will be very generous with their discount because of the business I bring. I pass much of the savings on to the clients and they are happy.

I can still get my 'commission,' usually 20%, and yet the clients get a great price for pressure washing.

PACKAGE ACCEPTANCE SERVICE

This may not generate instant cash but will be a big hit with current clients and prospects, and actually *saves you time*!

When people are away for months, packages may still be sent to their house. Clients will want them forwarded to them or placed inside or for their return.

Now you have to guess the date the package is due to arrive, go over to the property and check- oops, not yet. Next day you repeat, to find the box sitting in plain sight in the rain and wind. You put it inside. Three days later, your clients tell you they are expecting another package.

Extra time and trips that never earned you a penny...

Your Package Acceptance Service tells all your clients to use YOUR (business) address for the shipping arrival point. Packages now arrive on your doorstep, and you deliver them when you would normally go to the house for a survey instead of making an extra trip!

For clients, this means:

- No longer having to impose on the neighbors to get a package
- Not having to worry about the package being stolen, getting wet, or sitting outside in hot/cold temperatures.

This saves you time and money as opposed to making more money, but it's all good! Your clients will view this as a big benefit, while you are the one it benefits!

LANDSCAPING/TREE TRIMMING/LEAF REMOVAL

This vital service is important whether your business is in the North or South. In the South, many clients want their trees trimmed before the hurricane season. In the north, it's good to get trees trimmed before they are covered (and broken) by ice storms. In either case, snowbirds appreciate having someone they trust to get the job done. And again, having this done while they are away is a big selling point.

"Come home to play golf, not to supervise the landscapers" is one way to tell/sell this service.

SNOW REMOVAL

Ok, not a big idea if you live in Florida, but up North, this is a critical service. As noted in the book, *Leaving Your Home-ALONE*, untamed snow drifts are a signal to burglars and vandals the property is vacant.

Should there be a fire, snow also impedes emergency vehicles. Utility readers who are hurt on the property may have the right to sue. And sidewalks may actually be covered by city ordinances requiring clearing. For all these reasons, and a whole lot more, this is a service that snowbirds need.

This is also one that you should be able to contract easily. Then all you do is drive by and ensure the work was done and then bill your clients (adding in your management fee!)

CARPET/FLOOR CLEANING WHILE THE CLIENT IS AWAY

What better time to have the carpets cleaned, the tile and wood floor rejuvenated, then when the clients are gone?

You tell them the benefits:
- No waiting around all day for the person to arrive
- No waiting for carpets/flooring to dry
- It's clean when you come home
- It's guaranteed by YOU.

CAR/BOAT/AIRPLANE/MOTORCYCLE DETAILING

Have you ever had your car detailed? You lose its use for the entire day!

Instead offer this service, most like through a contractor, to your clients so they come home to a perfectly clean driving machine. And this can also apply to boats if one is left behind.

The best part is that you may be able to earn their trust enough to start an ongoing schedule for cleaning the 'toys.' Pre-scheduling an 'every spring and fall' cleaning detailing will even out the demand for your services and therefore your income.

HOUSE CLEANING SERVICE BEFORE ARRIVAL

They trudge in from thousands of miles away, tired and exhausted, hoping there is hot water for a shower, only to find the same dirty house they left. What can they do?

Your "Professional House Cleaning Before Your Arrival" offer may be just the ticket they need to make the leap and arrive home to a great looking property.

There are many ways to accomplish this one. If you already have a cleaning service, use that one. If not, ensure it is someone who is bonded and insured, in case something is broken or comes up missing...

DRYER VENT CLEANING

Know anyone who has ever cleaned his or her drier vent?

Except for the filter available from the front of the machine, the answer is probably NO. But you can offer this service.

All it takes is a few, readily available brushes, a little learning on the Internet, and you are ready.

Follow this link to see the kind of information you can pass to potential clients: *http://bit.ly/1fFvjat*

For a simple example of how to do it, try *http://www.wikihow.com/Clean-a-Clothes-Dryer-Vent*

HURRICANE SHUTTER INSTALLATION AND REMOVAL

Probably more common in the Southern states, hurricane shutters are sold for manual installation as well as the fancy electric versions. . Most people who own them couldn't install them if they tried.

And once they are installed, they must be removed when the threat has passed, another challenge most snowbirds don't want to do.

This is a service that can be offered whether they are in town or away. And all it usually takes is a drill and ladder.

AIRPORT PICK-UP/DROP OFF SERVICE

Many of your clients will be flying to their alternate homes. You can solve a big transportation problem with a simple little service that ensures they get to the airport and picked up from the airport on time.

I have used professional drivers with large SUVs for those leaving and arriving by private jet. And 'sedan services' that are competitively priced with taxis but much more clean and professional.

You may even have a small limo service in your town that will be willing to work with you on price. Do a google search or, if you still own them, use the yellow pages!

PROFESSIONAL HOME INVENTORY

Your clients mistakenly believe that their homeowner's insurance will cover anything that is lost. This is a myth. The insurance will only cover what they can PROVE they owned. And they must provide an *itemized listing*. A video alone won't cut it.

You can offer a complete home inventory of their property that includes the listing for them to send to their insurance agent!

A simple camera, light box, and software (free) will get you started. Then you give your clients a thumb drive or other digital storage device of the entire inventory for their safekeeping. This type of 'Once In Your Life" home inventory usually goes for $400-$1000 depending on the size of the house.

HOME INVENTORY DO-IT-YOURSELF KIT

Some people do not want to pay the $400-$1,000 for a professional home inventory. They mistakenly think they can take a few pictures and use that if there is a problem. WRONG.

Every insurance company requires a listing of the items, approximate date of purchase, receipts, purchase price, etc. No one wants to be fighting with this list in times of distress. So how can you help?

You can assemble your own 'Do-it-Yourself Home Inventory Kit'. For software, I recommend using 'Know Your Stuff' from the Insurance Information Institute. It's free. Then all you need are a camera (and most smartphones MAY work) and a light box kit to display all the items to be photographed and catalogued.

Portable kits can be bought for well less than $100 and includes everything you or your clients would need. A three day Friday through Sunday rental of $100 instead of the $400- $1000, may be appealing to your clients.

NOTES:

AUTHOR INSIGHT
SCAN WITH SMARTPHONE

or GO TO http://bit.ly/JJNgZS

SECTION 2: ADDITIONAL PRODUCTS

HOLIDAY FLOWERS

For any member of the family—Mom, spouse, daughter, etc., people who live in multiple homes can forget holidays. Birthdays, anniversaries, Mother's Day. Have you forgotten your anniversary? Oops.

You can solve this by offering a standing order for flowers to be delivered. I recommend you have cards for the 'sender' to fill out so that when the flowers arrive, they have a personal note from their loved one, not you!

WHOLE HOUSE WATER SHUTOFF VALVES

Most newer homes have a shutoff valve located in or near the garage. This valve shuts the water off from that point throughout the house.

But older homes do not have this type valve, but should. A whole house water shutoff means you can turn the water off when the homeowners are away, a great way to ensure there are no water leaks.

It is also great for troubleshooting water leaks by isolating the house. Plus you don't have to find the street vale to shut off water, possibly angering the water company who owns the valve.

Most plumbers can install a valve like this for less than $300. If properly presented to your clients, they will see the value immediately of this one time investment.

You get the advantage of having a single water shutoff; they get the security of knowing they can shut off the water to the entire house if there is ever a problem.

WHOLE HOUSE SURGE PROTECTOR

Have you had anything fried in a thunderstorm?

You know what a surge protector does, but did you know you could get one for the whole house? It is installed on the main circuit board by an electrician.

Now, one thing to keep in mind- these really only protect the appliances. *A whole-house surge protector cannot protect electronics, computers, etc.* But appliances—from garage door openers to freezers and fridges—are easily fried during a power surge.

Save your clients money with a one time install.

Some electric companies offer a similar device but then charge $10-12 EVERY month for the rest of their lives. What a rip! Here is your opportunity to help your clients save money and you get to keep some of it!

GOLF CART COUNTDOWN BATTERY CHARGER

It's not safe to leave golf cart batteries plugged into a charger all the time. Sure, there are supposed to be safety devices to reduce the risk, but I have see two major fires traced to charging the golf cart.

Thankfully, they were not under my control at the time.

But you still need to charge the golf cart without having the added trip back to the property to unplug the unit. The answer?

Sell the owner a 'countdown timer' that only charges for a certain period and then shuts off. And stays off until reset. This avoids the daily charging of most timers.

Here's how you do it.

NOTE: For this discussion, the timer is considered 'ON' when it allows electricity to flow through to the golf cart charger.

Look for a 15 Amp timer like the ones pictured below.

Not this type.

The simple ones with a dial and clips that you insert work best. (not the ones with tabs you pull out or push in like the one on the right).

To get the timer to work as a countdown only unit, simply remove the 'ON' tab(s), leaving only a single 'OFF' tab.

To use the timer: Manually turn the timer ON (usually a button or switch or knob). Then set the number of hours before the OFF tab stops the electricity.

Alternatively, you can set the current time and put the OFF tab on the time you want the timer to turn the electricity off.

It's a simple way to charge a golf cart without the fear of fire caused by daily charging. And most golf carts can be charged every other week or even monthly without a problem.

Carry spares in your vehicles and charge clients a round number that is about 50% more than you paid to allow for your costs.

CAR EMERGENCY KIT

Car emergency kits are not needed as often as in the past because of the increased reliability of vehicles. But hey, you never know, right? You can purchase a nice set or two and offer them for those who drive to their alternate home.

These also make a great enticement for new prospects to sign up with you. *"FREE Emergency Car Care Kit if you sign up with Billy's Home Watch Service before April 1st!!"*

MEDICAL EMERGENCY KIT

Bee stings, ant bites, minor cuts and scrapes-
where do you turn? Just like the Car emergency
kit, a portable Medical Emergency Kit is perfect for
those who travel. Keep it in the car and then bring
it into the house.

They hope it'll never be needed, but merely having
one will let them sleep better at night.

In your marketing material, consider pointing out
that the grandkids will get scraped and bruised
and grandma wants to be prepared!

MEDICAL GRADE FREEZER MONITORS

 If you live in the South, especially
Florida, you know what thunderstorms
can do. Florida is the Lightning Capitol of
the World. That means power outages.

So how do you know if the freezer you are checking
has defrosted and refrozen? A simple little tool
that costs less than $5 will let you know when a
freezer has gotten warm. This also works when a
freezer is failing and operates intermittently.

My favorite place to get these is:

www.tiptemp.com.
**(http://www.tiptemp.com/Products/Cost-
Effective-Fridge-Freezer-Room-Monitors)**

And don't forget to brag about these in your sales efforts, marketing, and newsletters. I called these my 'Health Saver Freezer Monitors' so my clients know these protect them from defrosted and refrozen food, which could contain deadly bacteria.

 You can sell them separately or use them to demonstrate how much better your service is from your competitors.

This is another great 'giveaway' for new clients, too.

WASHER HOSE UPGRADE

If you read the book *"Leaving Your Home - ALONE"* (highly recommended), you know washer hoses leaking or rupturing is a primary source of flooding. While your clients are just out to dinner, a burst hose can bleed 100 gallons a minute. 'How long will you be gone?'

Eliminate the threat almost entirely with upgraded hoses. You can buy airliner quality hoses that are reinforced with braided steel.

Some even have auto flow detectors that will shut down if they leak. (But I recommend just the simple braided hoses to avoid problems with the auto-shutoff.)

These hoses are virtually indestructible. Since most homeowners have NEVER replaced their washing machine hoses, this is a great investment. Have a set in your vehicle.

They come in different lengths, with 4 foot the recommended minimum.

They install easily, make you look professional, and you should be able to at least double your investment adding more profit to your pocket. These can also be used as an inducement to sign up with your service: "Free Steel braided Washer hose installation ($99 value) when you sign up this month..."

VEHICLE CARE/BATTERY MAINTENANCE SYSTEM

Do any of your clients leave a vehicle behind? Most do not recognize the damage that occurs to their engine and electronic components inside the engine when fuel is more than 60 days old. Plus batteries go dead.

And in Florida and other humid states, the interiors can grow fur due to mold.

Your solution should cover each of these areas with a fuel preservative/stabilizer, battery charger, and interior dehumidifier solution.

You can charge a single onetime fee of $149 and easily recover your costs plus let them keep the battery maintainer. Then each year charge a simple $39 fee to get the vehicle ready for the season. The yearly fee covers the cost of the fuel stabilizer and interior humidity chemicals plus a tidy little profit for you!

WATER SUPPLY LINE (RISER) UPGRADE SERVICE

The same supply lines that threaten to burst for the washing machine can be found wherever water goes from the wall or floor to the point where it is used. Toilets and faucets are the biggest culprits.

Replacing the cheap lines with the same type of steel braided lines can save hundreds of dollars from a single flooding. Once replaced, they are not even a thought.

AUTHOR INSIGHT
SCAN WITH SMARTPHONE

or GO TO http://bit.ly/1g15BNb

SECTION 3:
COMBINATIONS AND
LONG TERM MONEY
MAKER

SMALL BATTERY REPLACEMENT PLAN

Don't you hate it when your remote fails and you have to look for a battery? Or the garage door opener? Or that little clock on the mantle? Your clients hate that, too. Especially when they come home after 6 months and find that as a problem.

You can solve this with a simple "Battery Replacement Plan" that covers the most common items that fail.

SMOKE DETECTOR BATTERY/TESTING PLAN

When was the last time your smoke detectors were tested?"

Another approach is the 'How are you on ladders at night?' Your marketing would continue... because that battery-powered smoke detector will only start beeping, meaning it needs a fresh battery, when you are in bed at night. Imagine dragging the ladder out of the garage because your wife is getting a beepin' headache!

This approach is especially good if your clients are older- the most common subscribers to home watch services. Using this approach with the wife can also be useful. She doesn't want her husband on a ladder...

You can even send clients to a video, such as this one, which explains exactly how to do it. (http://www.youtube.com/watch?v=TGIazwYowTg).

NOTE: Don't worry that they will go and do it themselves- chances are very slim. Those that do would never use your additional service anyway!

Understanding exactly how to test their system is very important. If they have single, battery powered, units, they are only designed to get people out of the house when smoke is detected. A monitored system, on the other hand, will alarm each detector as well as call the alarm monitoring center and possibly the fire department.

You can learn it all online, and buy a can of 'smoke' from most hardware stores. The smoke will make you look professional, is the best way to test the units, and will only set you back about $10. You already own a ladder. Now just carry spare batteries, the 9V size is the most common.

An annual plan that charges $19.95 plus $7 per detector is well worth the price for many people. Ensure it includes battery changes every 6 months.

BILL PAYING SERVICE

If you have been in business long, you know the problem of homeowner's bills that went unpaid while they were away. They come home to the cable shutoff, insurance cancelled for the car, etc.

Or worse (Yes, I've seen it!) the water or electricity is turned off while they are gone. A simple solution is the offer of an 'Emergency bill paying service'. Designed to ensure nothing gets cancelled, you charge a minor fee of about $10 a month.

TOILET WARRANTY

Leaking toilets cost money. Many homeowners don't realize a toilet is leaking until the water bill comes.

Calling a plumber out to fix a single toilet can easily run $125. You can help your clients by offering a great service that guarantees the toilets will work—and fix them when they don't. All while you make money.

The 'guts' in a toilet tank are pretty simple. There are usually three main parts, some toilets may have a fourth. The three parts are the flapper valve, the handle, and the fill valve.

A complete kit that replaces all three (seldom necessary) is available at most big box hardware stores for less than $20. Plumbers will charge at least $75 PLUS a service call fee. You are already going to the house so you don't need to charge that fee.

You can tell your clients the regular price for a single repair could easily cost $125 for just a onetime visit, but you will warranty the toilet for one year at only $69 per toilet or $149 for all the toilets in the house.

Chances are everything will work fine.

But even if you have to replace one of the components you still have the money- in advance.

If you do end up replacing one of the parts, be sure to note the (plumber's rate) charge for the work on your client's monthly invoice, *and then the credit* underneath so that they see the benefit of your warranty.

If you want to see how it's done, simply google 'how to fix a toilet (flapper valve) (fill valve) or (handle)'. There are plenty of videos available for the less handy that will raise your confidence, get you more profit, and save the homeowner grief.

AC FILTER REPLACEMENT PLANS

How many people really replace their air conditioner filters on a regular basis?
Answer: Almost none.

So you can step in and solve the problem of slow air delivery, dust and pollen, and even possibly reduce the allergy issues with family members. It's pretty simple to do.

When you are the property, record the size of the filter. Most units will fall into about 6 different sizes. Offer the service on a quarterly or twice a year plan, using Better and BEST grade filters. DO NOT just use cheapies; it will ruin your reputation.

A good AC filter will run about $12 and a great one about $18. By offering the service as $49 for twice a year of good filters and $149 for quarterly changes of the best filter, you can save clients a lot of grief, actual money, wear and tear on the AC units, and doctor's visits.

Hint: Have you changed the filter on an AC unit and found a REALLY filthy filter? Save a sample in a plastic bag for use when talking about the AC filter service you offer.

THE "EASY LIVING" PACKAGE

With all these little plans, you can combine them into one or two 'Easy Living Options'. You combine different options into a package that is available for a nicer price.

For example, combining the toilet warranty and AC filter packages. Or also add the smoke detector testing and battery plan.

Combining makes them more attractive and since you are already at the property for one plan, there are no additional costs in time or gas to get there for another plan. While you are changing the AC filter, you can do the smoke detector batteries.

WHOLE HOUSE YEAR AROUND PLAN

The Whole Enchilada, the whole nine yards—name it what you want. But it includes doing the common items that can break in the course of the year.

A whole house monthly maintenance plan spreads the year's required preventive maintenance over 12 months and can include:

- Plumbing service including drain cleaning
- Clean out gutters
- Tighten all electrical outlets
- Changing out bad light bulbs
- Smoke detector testing and battery changes
- Garage door servicing using yourself or a professional
- AC servicing by a professional
- Fridge cooler cleaning (older units with exposed grids, especially those on the bottom)
- Oil all hinges (all doors- interior, exterior, kitchen, etc) to prevent squeaks
- Tighten all door knobs (interior/exterior, cabinets)
- Adjust door closers
- Install/remove storm windows and screens
- Check water in batteries for all vehicles
- Drain water heater once a year

- Dishwasher cleaner, washing machine cleaner
- Driveway weeds
- Dishwasher cleaner
- Washing Machine cleaner
- Lint removal of dryers/hoses/lines
- Golf cart batteries- adding water
- Lots of other ideas

You can offer this as part of a monthly billing to 'level out' the higher seasonal payments with the off-season. I charge $150 a month for the home watch portion.

For year around service, I charge $50 for the monthly visits during the off-season. Since most of my clients are gone for 6 months and home for the other six, that works out to an even $100 a month for 'Year Around Service".

Clients will then see you as the 'go-to person' for other needs where you arrange the service and collect a tidy management fee!

HOW TO IMPLEMENT THESE IDEAS

None of these additional services will ever make money unless your clients- and potential clients- know about them.

Consider these methods:

- ✓ Pick a service a month and note it in your newsletter. As soon as you get a client into one of the programs, congratulate them in the newsletter.
- ✓ Design a brochure for one or more of the services.
- ✓ Use a mini-booklet/catalog that covers all of them, one per page. Send it out to all clients and prospects.
- ✓ Offer one of the services "Free with Signup or Renewal"
- ✓ Have a link on your website to the additional services section. I don't recommend a lot of detail or pricing here as many unscrupulous competitors will try to copy everything you do. (Ask me how I know!) When they offer a cheap alternative, it makes yours look expensive, even though it is better.
- ✓ Time your offers to the time of the season. A simple 'do you need us to arrange transportation to/from the airport' is a great question at the departure/return time of the year.

I use a handout that lists all our additional
services. It is available for potential clients to see,
whenever I do a home show or other marketing
effort, gets quoted in literature I use, and costs less
than $100 for enough to last a couple years.

NOTES:

FINALLY: HOW CAN I DO IT ALL?

You may be overwhelmed just thinking of all the ideas in this book. The most common question is: How could I ever do it all?

The answer is quite simple: you can't!

You may choose to do one of the ideas yourself, such as the home inventory or pressure washing. But you can't do everything as the business owner. There are only so many hours in the day. And you don't want to get burned out. You will never have time to get your business working if you spend time doing all the work yourself.

The key is getting qualified sub-contractors. And they must be:

INSURED

You need to ask immediately if they have insurance. Then ask them to send it to you. This is very common.

You keep this paperwork in a file for your own records as your home watch insurer will want to know you are checking. If there is a problem with them providing it, drop them immediately.

It may be a fly-by-night, cash only, service. You will thank me when you do this. But many will ignore this advice and lose money, clients, and good reputation before all the damage is actually done...

RELIABLE

With my business, I use the 'two strikes rule', especially for appointments. If we agree to meet at a property at 10 a.m. and the contractor is not there by 10:10, I leave.

I call them and tell them my time is important. If they can't be on time, maybe we shouldn't be doing business. That usually gets their attention and our relationship gets on track and stays that way.

But if it happens twice, without a courtesy call saying they are running late, I refuse to do business with them. They fail to remember that the person paying the money is the boss! So reliability is very important since my properties are all over the county!

GUARANTEED

I guarantee the work that I arrange to my clients. So, if I arrange a pressure wash, and the owner is not happy, the client only needs to work with me, not the contractor.

Because of that, I have high demands for my contractors- and not everyone is willing or able to meet those demands. One is their assurance of return calls until the owner is happy.

I don't have time to be running out and chasing contractors for less than great work. Those contractors who want work will get a lot of business from me- unless they cause me more headaches!

REASONABLY PRICED

This is usually not an issue, but you need to investigate what the local area fees are for the service you will be contracting. When I got started, a pressure washing service gave me a quote for a house of $1700. Another quoted $550.

When I approached both and asked them to clarify what was included, they were the same. A little research saved me a ton of money.

In another case, I researched and found a registered and licensed plumber who would put in a whole house water shutoff for about $250. That was less than the competition because I agreed they would do all the ones I ever needed at that price.

PROFESSIONAL LOOKING

The last thing you want is someone going to your client's property looking like a burglar casing the joint! True professionals have clean vehicles, nicely signed, and usually some form of uniform.

WILLING TO BILL YOU OR TAKE YOUR CREDIT CARD

NOT expecting you to carry around cash or a checkbook. There are plenty of legitimate businesses that know better; find and use them.

When you hire a contractor, YOU set the rules – or find someone else.

HOW DO YOU BILL FOR OUTSIDE WORK, MARK?

I add an additional 20%. I have advised my clients ahead of time that I add 20% for all services up to $2,000, 15% from $2,000-4,000, and 10% for anything above that figure.

WHAT HAVE I USED CONTRACTORS FOR?

- ➤ New roofs, roof repairs
- ➤ Kitchen makeover, dishwasher, disposal installations
- ➤ Central air conditioning unit repair and replacements
- ➤ Whole house shut off valves, Garage door opener installations, carpet cleaning, appliance repairs, sprinkler repairs, etc, etc.

When you guarantee your contractor's work, and agree to take liability for the work, most clients realize the value of the time and risk they save. If they would prefer to sit around all day waiting for the guy they called to get there, let them do it!

The smart ones will see the value of using you to handle the hassles in their busy lives.

SUMMARY

As you build your Home Watch business, you will have opportunities to sell more. Buyers of any service develop a trust and reliance on that service.

When buyers see other opportunities of a similar type from a provider, they will use that provider (YOU!) if they already trust you and love the results.

This book gives you proven ideas that I have used in my business. Good luck in yours!

NOTES:

AUTHOR INSIGHT
SCAN WITH SMARTPHONE

or GO TO http://bit.ly/1hUVkn4

BONUS SECTION: WHAT DO YOU DO IN THE OFF-SEASON?

Everyone in this business has a slow period. What do you do during this time? Relax? Goof off? Marketing?

Here's what successful home watch business owners need to do:

The 5 'R' Strategy:
Review, Reassess,
Reinvigorate, Referrals,
Remind

REVIEW THE PAST SEASON

In spite of your best efforts, things went wrong. But a lot also went right.

It may be things you forget, items you heard were very appreciated, while others went less noticed. Now is the time to look at every property, every client, and consider what could have made the experience even better for them.

Then put system in place to ensure those problems don't repeat. And solidify the system that brought the most praise.

No season will ever be perfect, but you should be continually improving.

REASSESS

What can you do better? Different? How can you differentiate yourself from other services? Unlike reviewing what went right and wrong, this is a look from the outside to determine what overall change to the business will make your job easier, clients happier, etc.

Maybe you tried something new. Decide whether to continue.

For example, I had a grocery list on my website that clients could check off items they wanted at the house before their arrival home. It was a very comprehensive list.

After 2 seasons I realized most people only want a couple basics, like milk, bread, and cereal to get started. It changed the whole way I presented that feature.

REINVIGORATE.

Look for ways to make your job easier. Now that you have a chance to breathe, how can you make changes to your business to reduce the time and effort required to service your clients?

Consider:

Automation: use software or hardware to save time. Some of my favorites are using FormStack (**www.formstack.com**) to make survey checklists that can be completed on a smart phone, then automatically sent to your office email. Saves tons of time and paper.

Methods: Refine how you do your walk-throughs/surveys. If you accepts checks (I personally recommend only credit cards), find a way to deposit them without having to make trips to the bank.

REFERRALS

Now is the best time to get those needed referrals and testimonials. Your clients are home, they have just had a great arrival (hopefully!) and they are pleased to talk about it.

Choose written (like a questionnaire) or free- hand letters or email. Also choose phone calls or video. You can record and edit phone calls, you can ask them to call and leave a message (very non invasive).

Now is a great time to implement the 'Five Around' marketing method. After you get the referral from a client, send it, along with some marketing literature, to each of the five neighbors around your client. Even if they are not snowbirds, they may bring the conversation up with your client and refer others.

REMIND

Remind them you are there. Use a monthly newsletter, email or paper (I prefer paper), use thank you cards, Thanksgiving or Christmas cards, Coffee cakes in the middle of the off season, Special invitations to events (local plays or theater, special offers that only previous clients receive, etc.

People will forget when they do not hear from you. Reminding them can be as simple as a postcard asking them to confirm the date of their departure. But other methods that don't directly have a sales tone should also be used.

The off-season is a great time to fine tune while the demands of the business are lighter. Using the 5R Strategy give you an outline for making real improvements that benefit your clients, your time, and your profit!

WANT TO IMPRESS YOUR CLIENTS WITH A GIFT?

Giving them a copy of my book, *Leaving Your Home-ALONE* (available at **www.Amazon.com**), <u>for their *other* house</u> can make you the hero. It will open their eyes to the dangers of leaving any property empty as well as let them know what a magnificent job you are doing.

It's full of stories, solutions, and is designed to let them make a personalized checklist that is just for their home-away-from-home.

Don't worry that they will try to do it themselves. The book makes it very obvious that every empty house needs a home watch service.

Tell them this is a gift for them to give to the 'other' service managing their seasonal home. They will be impressed with you- and with your generosity and caring for their lives and the other place they call home.

AUTHOR INSIGHT
SCAN WITH SMARTPHONE
or GO TO http://blt.ly/1a1fqdE

OTHER BOOKS AND RESOURCES FROM THE AUTHOR

BOOKS

Leaving Your Home-ALONE
- A step-by-step guide to leaving your property empty for months at a time.

17 Days to Your Own Profitable Home Watch Business
A guide to establishing your own business in less than 3 weeks

Both available on Amazon.com

Look for these additional resources soon:

BOOKS

Blow Away the Competition in Your Home Watch Business

How to differentiate your service from all the others while charging higher prices! Do you constantly get phone calls with just one question: "How much to do you charge?"

That's because prospects cannot tell the difference between you and 'low-end Larry' who has no clue what he is doing, is not insured, and couldn't spot a problem if his life depended on it. You must educate clients and make your home watch service stand out.

This book is jammed packed with the keys to making your business so much higher than your competition it will be beyond comparison!

DVDs

These DVDs are the secrets that Mark has kept to himself for years. No one else is willing to 'let it all out'. Now you can get copies of everything that Mark used to make HomeWatchValet the leader in the industry.

DVD101: HomeWatchValet's Award Winning Marketing

Copies of over 50 pieces of marketing materiel that can be adapted to any Home Watch Service.

These are the same pieces that won Mark and HomeWatchValet "Marketer of the Year" finalist from GKIC, a 25,000 member marketing group.

Looking for a magazine ads, brochure, direct mail letter? There are multiple examples of each in this CD. Even includes a copy of our 'catalog' of services, which instantly sets you above the competition.

Your bonus with this CD is digital samples of the "Your Florida HOME" paper newsletter which always gets client raves—even from the grumpy ones! This is a simple to do format using PowerPoint, but you can use any method that works for you.

And it can be as simple as 4 pages, much of which you can get from other sources.

Now you have access to these newsletters to copy the format, ideas- anything you like. I promise once you do it, it becomes simple- and makes a huge difference in your income.

DVD102: Every Checklist/Form for Any Home Watch Situation

You could spend hours guessing what to look at in a property, or trying to copy Internet checklists.

Instead save the hours of work (and the risk of getting it wrong!) by using the proven checklists that keeps my clients properties safe.

Opening, Closing, Post Storm, regular surveys, Condos—how to customize a checklist for each property. It's all here, including guidance for a key security system that will protect you from lawsuits and save you money.

The bonus with this CD is checklists/forms for office use:
- ➢ -New client information gathering checklist
- ➢ -New client steps to be done in the office
- ➢ -Closing out a client account checklist
- ➢ -Form for billing additional work
- ➢ PLUS A Whole Lot More

DVD103: Every Tool I Use- and Why

HomeWatchValet's premium service reputation was earned by using an array of tools. Too many to list, now there is a CD that covers more than 80 items incorporated over the first 5 years as we refined what was essential to keep a property in tip-top shape.

You can make the mistakes yourself- and pay for it with angry clients and hundreds of repair bills, or just but this CD and pick and choose exactly what you need!

These DVDs are available directly from the author for $97 US/$110 International each postage paid. Or all three for $259US/$299 Int'l. Use the order form on the following page.

If you would like notice of future books and CDs, send an email to the author at **Mark@TakeControlMarketing.com.** Your email will only be used to notify you when new products are available and will not be used or sold for any other purpose.

Want to become a local celebrity?

Are you ready to become a published author?

Do you want the instant **respect** and **recognition** that comes with having your own book- with your name and picture on the cover?

Your book will bring _new business; establish you as an expert; gives instant credibility with prospects_; and makes an incredible marketing handout—just like the book you are reading now!

It's simple with the *39PageGuideBooks* proven system. All you do is provide about 20 pages of 8 ½ x 11 information your potential clients and prospects want to know.

We do all the rest

- 30 minute free consultation to get your started
- Full-color cover design
- Interior formatting in 6x9 size
- Printing
- Kindle® E-book & CreateSpace Print formatting
- ISBN & Library of Congress number assignment

- Amazon.com placement
- 25 FREE books

Your own promotional book helps you become a celebrity in your town, in your business, and costs less than $4 per book after the initial setup.

Contact *39PageGuideBooks* to become a published author in less than 60 days!

Email: **MyOwnBook@39PageGuideBooks.com** for more information.

ORDER FORM

NOTE: Order books on www.Amazon.com.

Make Checks/Money Order out to *"Take Control Marketing"*

Item	Name	Qty	Price	
DVD101	MARKETING		$97 EA*	
DVD102	CHECKLISTS		$97 EA*	
DVD103	EVERY TOOL AND WHY		$97 EA*	
DVDSET	ALL 3 DVDs		$259*	
	* Includes shipping			

Add *__International__* Shipping ($13 per CD or $30 per set)

TOTAL Check/MO   _____

Ship to:

Name _____

Address _____

City _____

State _____

Zip _____

email _____

Enclose check or money order and MAIL to:
Take Control Marketing, 1866 Seclusion Dr, Port Orange Fl 32128

ABOUT THE AUTHOR

Mark Mehling is a serial entrepreneur who started HomeWatchValet in 2005. After retiring from the military, he continues to fly as a commercial pilot, and sees the world through the lens of marketing.

Using the marketing materials and results from HomeWatchValet, he was "Marketer of the Year" finalist for Glazer-Kennedy Insider's Circle, now GKIC, a 25,000+ group of business owners from all over the globe intent on growing their businesses by following the methods of Dan Kennedy.

As a trained copywriter, he also is a member of the American Writers and Artists (AWAI) Circle of Success. His book, *"Leaving Your Home-ALONE,"* is the leading publication for information on leaving property empty for months at a time.

In his business, HomeWatchValet, Mr. Mehling still has some of his original clients from his first year in 2005. Most of those clients whose property he no longer watches have moved, sold their home, or passed away.

Mr. Mehling started HomeWatchValet in 2005. While walking his beautiful dog, an Akita named Zoie, he came upon an empty home with water seeping from the garage. The neighbors knew nothing. No one knew how to contact the homeowner. No one had a key.

Mr. Mehling and the neighbors watched helplessly as water came from the garage. When someone finally broke a window on a door at the side of the garage, they gained access only to find a broken water softener line had flooded the 'sunken' living room.

After filling up, it started draining to the garage where it slowly went down the driveway. There was at least $20,000 damage according to a friend who was involved with the cleanup.

Mr. Mehling knew there had to be a better way. Thus was born Home Watch Valet.

Mark Mehling is also the author of *Leaving Your Home-ALONE*, a step-by-step guide to leaving a property vacant for months at a time, available on Amazon.com.

Made in the USA
San Bernardino, CA
20 August 2015